Worlds Apart:
The Twentieth Century

STEVE BUXTON

Hodder & Stoughton

A MEMBER OF THE HODDER HEADLINE GROUP

Acknowledgements

The front cover shows a painting of 'Lenin on a Panzerwagon' reproduced courtesy of AKG Photo, London.

Alfred Kantor and The Weiner Library p. 40 right; Popperfoto p. 4 bottom, p. 27 bottom left; Novosti p. 5 bottom, p. 9 right, p. 45 left; Musée de l'Armée p. 7; AKG Photo, London p. 9, p. 19 left; Hulton Deutsch Collection Limited, London p. 13, p. 24, p. 27 top left, p. 27 bottom right, p. 29 bottom left and top right, p. 30, p. 32 left and right, p. 47 top right; Advertising Archives p. 15 left, p. 47 middle right; Topham Picture Point p. 15 right; Imperial War Museum p. 17 top, p. 26 left, p. 27 left, p. 33 left, p. 34, p. 35; Bildarchiv Preussischer Kulturbesitz p. 17 bottom, p. 18 left, p. 25 left and right, p. 39, p. 40 left, p. 41; The Weiner Library p. 18 right; Robert Hunt Library, London p. 26 top right; Daily Mail p. 26 bottom right; Colorsport p. 47 bottom right.

This book is dedicated with respect to my parents and their generation.

British Library Cataloguing in Publication Data
A catalogue entry for this title is available from the British Library

ISBN 0 340 644087

First published 1997
Impression number 10 9 8 7 6 5 4 3 2 1
Year   2002 2001 2000 1999 1998 1997

Typeset by Fakenham Photosetting Ltd, Fakenham, Norfolk.
Printed in Great Britain for Hodder & Stoughton Educational, a division of Hodder Headline Plc, 338 Euston Road, London NW1 3BH by Scotprint, Musselburgh, Scotland.

Contents

1

War and Peace in the Twentieth Century

civilians atomic bomb co-operate

There have been many terrible wars in the 20th century. Millions of people were killed, soldiers, sailors airmen and civilians. Many new weapons were invented. Poison gas, rockets, missiles, and, most fearsome of all, the atomic bomb.

Hiroshima is a city in Japan. It was destroyed by one atomic bomb in 1945

Many good things too have happened in the 20th century. New medical cures were invented. People began to explore space. American and Russian spacecraft met above the earth in November 1995 to show that it is possible for countries to co-operate.

Russians and Americans meet in space in 1995

TALKING POINTS

1 For what reasons do you think countries fight wars against each other?

2 There have been many new inventions in the twentieth century. Make a list of as many as you can think of. Divide your list into two. On one side put those things you think have improved people's lives. On the other side put those which have made life worse.

Compare your lists with other people's lists. How do they agree/disagree?

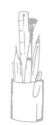

WORKFILE

1 Use the information from your lists. Design a display called 'War and Peace in the Twentieth Century'. You might spend some time looking through the rest of this book to get some extra ideas for your display.

2 *What Was the Great War?*

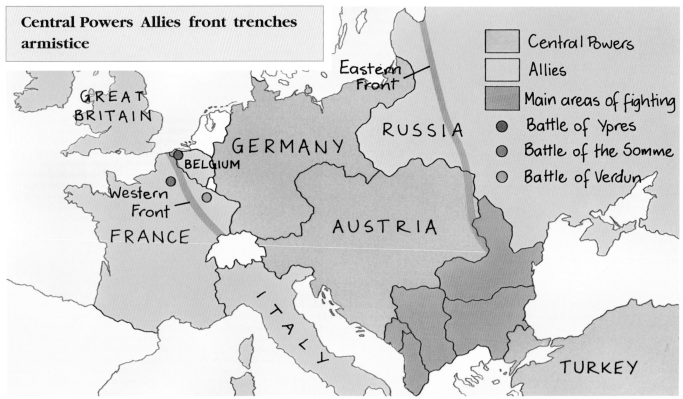

Central Powers Allies front trenches armistice

Source A Europe in 1914

The First World War started in 1914. It became known as 'The Great War'. No war in history had ever been fought on this scale.

The map above shows which countries fought each other. On one side were the Central Powers, mainly Germany and Austria. On the other side were the Allies, mainly France, Britain, Italy and Russia. The U.S.A. joined the Allies in 1917. A few weeks later Russia left the war.

There were three main areas of fighting: the Western Front, the Eastern Front and the Balkans.

Why Was it a World War?

Many European countries had Empires at this time. Though most of the fighting took place in Europe the war affected people all over the world. For example, soldiers from India, Canada, Australia and New Zealand came to Europe to fight on Britain's side.

The Western Front

At the start of the war German armies moved into France and Belgium. They were stopped by the British and French armies. There were huge battles at the Marne and Ypres. Then both sides 'dug in'. The soldiers dug trenches to protect themselves.

Source B Soldiers in a trench

On the 'Western Front' the area of fighting hardly moved for four years. Both sides attacked each other at different times. Wave after wave of soldiers were killed trying to attack enemy trenches. Attacks nearly always failed. In 1916 the Germans attacked the French at Verdun. The battle lasted for 11 months. 680 thousand soldiers died but neither side really won. The British attacked on the Somme in 1916. The battle raged for months. Thousands of soldiers died but the British only managed to capture a few hundred metres of enemy ground. There were many other battles like these.

The End of the War

In 1918 the Germans started a massive attack. For a while they were winning but they were short of food and supplies. After many bitter battles the Allies started to push the Germans back. At last they captured large areas of land. In Germany many people were starving. They wanted the war to end. Both sides agreed to stop fighting and an armistice was signed. At 11 o'clock on 11 November 1918 the Great War ended.

WORKFILE

1 Copy and complete this table. Write in the names of the countries who fought for each side. Write a sentence to explain what happened to Russia and the U.S.A.

Table 1

Allies	Central Powers

2 Copy and complete the paragraph below. Use these words to complete the sentences: were Europe side Allies from ended other move

The Great War started in 1914. The _____ fought against the Central Powers. Soldiers _____ around the world came to fight in _____. The area of fighting did not _____ much on the Western Front. Neither _____ was strong enough to force the _____ back even though there _____ many massive battles. The Armistice _____ the war on 11.11.1918 at 11 a.m.

Did the Two Sides Make Peace?

treaty reparations

When the fighting stopped in 1918, the two sides had to agree peace terms. Leaders from Britain, France and the U.S.A. met at Versailles in France. Their side had won. They decided what the peace treaty should say.

France had the biggest say. The French knew what they wanted. Germany had invaded their country. Large areas of France had been destroyed. Millions of people had been killed. France wanted revenge. Germany should pay large sums of money in 'reparations' to repair the damage. Germany should be kept weak, too weak to threaten France ever again.

German leaders did not like the Treaty of Versailles which they were forced to sign. The war was over, but was there really peace between France and Germany?

Source C Consequences of the Treaty of Versailles

TALKING POINTS

The Treaty of Versailles did not lead to a lasting peace in Europe.

1 Why do you think it led to further trouble?

2 If you had written it, what would you have done differently?

WORKFILE

1 Look at the picture below. Suppose a French and German person made these statements about the Treaty of Versailles in 1919. Work out who said what. Copy and complete the table using the statements in the picture.

	The Treaty of Versailles What did they say?
French opinions	
German opinions	

Why Did Russia Stop Fighting?

peasants **Tsar** **luxurious** **Communists**
Lenin rifles **deserted** rebelled
revolution

Russia was still a backward country in 1914. In some cities there were factories and jobs, but Russia was a huge country. Many Russians were peasants. They worked on the land but were very poor. Often they hardly had enough to eat. Tsar Nicholas II ruled Russia. Unlike his subjects, he lived a very luxurious life.

Source A Tsar Nicholas II

The Communists

Some Russians were unhappy about the way Tsar Nicholas ran the country. They wanted a better life for the people. Lenin led one group who demanded change. They were

Communists. They believed that Russia's wealth should be shared out more equally. Peasants should have a share of the land. Workers should have a share of the factory where they worked. No one in Russia would be very rich and no one in Russia would be very poor. Everyone would be more equal.

Source B Lenin speaking from an armoured car

Russia was having a hard time in the Great War. Things were so bad that soldiers had to share rifles. Thousands deserted and went home. Some rebelled against the Tsar. Russia faced a revolution.

WORKFILE

Write a sentence to answer these questions.

1 Who was the Russian ruler in 1914?

2 What did the peasants do for a living?

3 Which group of people said that wealth should be shared out equally?

4 Who was their leader?

5 Why did Russian soldiers desert?

1. 1916. Eastern Front. Russian soldiers are deserting.

How can we fight a war with no rifles?

Our families in Russia need us to farm the land.

They're even more hungry than us. Let's go home.

2. St Petersburg. Russia February 1917.
Starving people riot in the streets. The Tsar and his family flee from their Winter Palace.

3. This way your highness.

4. March 1917.
The Tsar abdicates.
Who will rule now?

5. Lenin makes plans with the 'Red Guard'- armed men and women who will fight for communism.

LONG LIVE THE REVOLUTION

When the time is right we will be ready.

6. 25ᵗʰ October 1917.
Red Guards seize control of key buildings like the Winter Palace.

Move over we are in control now.

7. Lenin meets German war leaders February 1918.

We agree to stop fighting. You give us some of Russia's land.

It's a deal.

TALKING POINTS

1 Why do you think many Russians were prepared to follow the Communists? Why did many people disagree with them?

2 Why did Lenin make peace with Germany?

WORKFILE

1 Work in pairs. One person works for the Red Army in 1919 and one for the White Army. Design a poster. Tell people about the death of the Tsar and his family. When you compare posters they should give a very different view of the same event. Use these words to help you. Choose which ones you use carefully.

murdered   killed   death   great leader   tyrant luxury   starving

2 Suppose you were a speech writer working for Lenin in 1916. Write a short speech. Explain what you believe is wrong with Russia and what you want to do about it.

3 These newspaper headlines tell the story of the Russian Revolution but in the wrong order. Make your own copy of the table. Sort them into the right order. First fill in the missing words. Choose from this list: with   family   Civil   Eastern   seize   ruler   riots

Table 1

1916	Communists kill Tsar and ___.
February 1917	Red Army win ___ War. Lenin is ___ of all Russia.
October 1917	Russian Troops mutiny on ___ Front.
February 1918	Red Guards ___ Winter Palace.
July 1918	Food ___ in St Petersburg.
1920	Russia makes peace ___ Germany.

4 *The 1920s and 1930s*

The period after the Great War was a troubled one. There were fewer jobs and for many people wages were poor. Trade Unions led many strikes to protest about pay and long working hours. This role play tells the story of Britain's worst ever strike, the General Strike of 1926. It started with a fight between the mine owners and coal miners. Other countries were selling their coal cheaper than British coal. Mine owners wanted to cut their costs so they could compete. The miners were told to work longer for less money. They refused and went on strike. Soon other unions joined in to help the miners. Would Britain come to a standstill? The government had to do something.

Before You Start

Form a group of four players. Each person chooses one character to follow. Read about your character. Tell the others about yourself. Prepare a chart like the one on page 13. Choose from:

Megan Davies

Your husband, Thomas, is a miner in South Wales. He needs to work to support your family of six children. If he strikes you will have no wages to live on. But your family is hard pressed. You can't manage on his wages now,

and the owners want to cut pay. It's time to take a stand.

David Rees

Mine owner. No one buys the coal from your pit. It is too expensive. You need to cut costs. It's true the miners have a hard job, but at least they have a job. They will have to take a pay cut or lose it.

A.J. Cook

Miners' trade union leader. You know the miners can't afford a pay cut. If they all fight together they can stand up to the mine owners. The mine owners will lose out if there is a strike. They won't have any coal to sell. Other workers may join in to help the miners.

Edith Barnett

Middle-class woman from London. You don't know much about mines or miners. You have heard that the miners have a hard life but they don't have to do the job, do they? They don't have the right to hold the country to ransom.

How To Play

a At the start of each round one person in your group reads out the news.

b Decide how your character will react to the news. Discuss it with the rest of your group.

Score chart

Round	Davies	Rees	Cook	Barnett
1				
2				
3				
4				
5				

c Copy the score chart. Write a score for each person on your score chart.

1 = very unhappy 2 = unhappy

3 = not bothered 4 = pleased

5 = very pleased

d Go on to the next round.

e At the end, add up the scores for each person. What do the totals show you about different people's attitudes to the strike?

Here is the News

1 *30 April 1926*. Miners Strike! Mines all over the country are shut down. Union demands 'Not a penny off the pay, not a minute on the day.'

2 *3 May 1926*. General Strike starts today. Millions of workers go on strike to support the miners. Britain grinds to a halt.

3 *4 May 1926*. Prime Minister speaks out. Stanley Baldwin attacks strikers. The army moves in to get food supplies moving. Volunteers drive buses in London. Reports of clashes between police and strikers.

4 *12 May 1926*. General Strike is over. Union leaders accept defeat and call off action. Only miners remain on strike.

5 *November 1926*. Miners' strike is over. Last few remaining strikers drift back to work. Forced back by cold and hunger they accept longer hours and less pay.

TALKING POINTS

1 Do you think strikes are a good thing or a bad thing?

2 Why do you think the miners lost in 1926?

WORKFILE

Write a newspaper report for 12 May 1926. Explain what the strike was about and how it has come to an end.

Source A A member of the public drives a tram during the strike

Other countries too had problems in the 1920s. Germany was worst hit, struggling to pay reparations owed after the war. Serious inflation was a big problem. German people found that their money bought less and less as prices shot up. Then it got out of hand. By 1923 German money was worth next to nothing. This table shows how much German people had to pay for one egg. People carried paper money around in sacks. Germany was bankrupt.

	1914	1918	1922	AUG 1923	NOV 1923
	0.1	0.25	200	5 thousand	90 million
How much did an egg cost in German Marks					

The U.S.A. went through a boom period in the 1920s. Factories did well. There were plenty of jobs. But by 1929 things were slowing down. America's Stock Market is on Wall Street, New York. People bought shares in American companies. Some spent millions of dollars. In October 1929 Wall Street 'crashed'. The value of shares fell rapidly. Many people lost a fortune as the shares they owned became worth less and less. In the next few years America suffered the Great Depression. Factories closed. Farmers found it hard to sell their goods. People lost their jobs. Thousands travelled around the county looking for work.

Things were not all bad though in the 1920s and 1930s. Some parts of Britain did quite well. Richer people could afford some of the new inventions which were coming on the market, like cars, washing machines and vacuum cleaners. There were new factories needed and new jobs for people who made these new consumer goods.

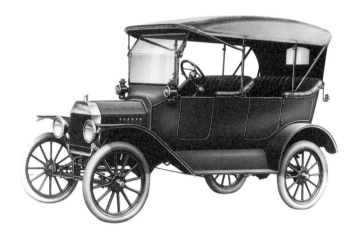

Source B A Model T Ford

Many car makers copied the new way Henry Ford made cars in America. His factory made cars much more quickly and cheaply. They were the first car makers to use a production line. Ford car workers took their place beside a big conveyor belt. As the car came past on the belt each worker fixed something to it, for example, a steering wheel. Then the next car would come along and the worker fixed a steering wheel to that one. In 1929, one Model T Ford dropped off the end of the 'Magic Belt' every three minutes. Thanks to these new methods more people could afford to own a car in the 1930s.

Source C Model T Fords on the production line

TALKING POINTS

Study these Rover and Electrolux adverts. What do they tell us about the past?

1 a Who do you think the adverts are aimed at? Which characters on page 12 might buy a car or cleaner. How do the adverts appeal to these people?

b What can you learn about fashion in the 1930s from these adverts.

c 'Times were hard in the 1930s.' Do the adverts prove this is a lie?

WORKFILE

1 Write a sentence or two about the following. Use the words in brackets to help you:
• Germany 1923 • America 1929
• Ford's Magic Belt
(problem   inflation   German Mark   worthless   bankrupt/Wall Street Crash   shares   falling prices   lost fortunes/cars   production line   cheaply affordable)

2 Design an advert for the 1929 model T Ford. Decide how you will appeal to your target audience.

Source D Advert for an Electrolux vacuum cleaner

Source E Advert for a Rover car

Why Was Hitler The Führer?

Nazi Führer **racist** unemployed **recovery**

In 1933 Adolph Hitler became the ruler of Germany. His 'Nazi' Party ruled until 1945. What did the Nazis stand for? Why did the German people follow Hitler as their leader or 'Führer'?

In the early 1930s millions of Germans were unhappy. Their country had suffered badly since the end of the Great War. Many people were desperate. They had no job. They had no money. The Nazis offered hope to many German people. They promised to give Germany back its pride. They said they were Germany's last hope (see Source A).

The Nazis blamed Jews for Germany's problems. They said Jews had caused Germany to lose the Great War. They said Jews were getting rich while other Germans starved. Some Germans believed the Nazis were telling the truth, even though many German Jews were also starving. The picture below shows some Nazi beliefs.

TALKING POINTS

1 Which of Hitler's ideas do you agree and disagree with?

2 Which ideas are likely to cause trouble with other countries like Britain and France? Why?

3 Why did Hitler need to blame Germany's problems on people like the Jews rather than other Germans?

4 Do you think the Nazis were 'racist'?

● At the end of the Great War Germany got a bad deal. The Treaty of Versailles should be cancelled.

● The Germans are the 'Master Race'.

● The 'Master Race' needs more land. Then it can grow bigger and richer.

● The Jews are a separate race. They are the enemy of all true Germans.

Source A 'Our last hope'

One German explained why he and many others joined the Nazi Party.

Source B

'Hitler persuaded us. Instead of hopeless unemployment Germany could move towards recovery.'

By 1938 the Nazis said they had put Germany back on its feet. People were found jobs. Some of them built new motorways, the first in Europe.

Source C Building a new German motorway

There were other new jobs too, making planes, tanks and submarines. Hitler was rebuilding Germany's armed forces. Less people were out of work after the Nazis took over (see Source D). In 1932 Hitler had claimed that he was Germany's last hope. By 1938 many Germans were happy with the way things were going.

Source D German unemployment

1933	6.0 million
1934	3.7 million
1935	not available
1936	2.5 million
1937	1.8 million
1938	1.0 million

WORKFILE

1 Suppose you are a Jew living in Germany in 1932. The Nazi Party see you as their enemy. Design a leaflet for the election. Tell people not to vote for Hitler. Explain why you disagree with Nazi ideas.

2 Use the figures in Source D.
   a Draw a bar graph. Show the changes in unemployment levels in Germany between 1933 and 1938.
   b Write a sentence or two. Explain what the graph is showing.

3 Write a paragraph to sum up what you have learned about Hitler and the Nazis. Use these words to help you.
Hitler leader Nazi ruler Germany desperate blamed Jews 'Master Race' hope recovery

How Did the Nazis Persuade People?

persuade propaganda rallies invention

The Nazi Party was very good at persuading people. They were propaganda experts. Hitler was a brilliant speech maker. People who heard him were won over by the power of his words. Nazi leaders planned huge rallies. Sometimes Hitler spoke to crowds of one hundred thousand people.

Source E A Nazi Nuremberg rally

A new invention allowed Nazis to persuade millions more people in their own homes.

Here is the Nazi news followed by a talk from the Führer himself.

The Nazis used radio to carry their message to the German people. They gave strict orders about what went out on the air

The Nazis hoped to brainwash people. They wanted to control the way people thought. One Nazi leader wrote:

Source F 'Through the radio and loudspeaker the thoughts of 80 million people were controlled by one man.'

Much Nazi propaganda was aimed at children. The Nazis gave orders about what children should be taught at school and what books they should read. Source G is from a Nazi children's book. One person is meant to be from the German 'Master Race', the other is meant to show a Jew.

Source G From a Nazi children's book

TALKING POINTS

1 Study Source E. What does it tell you about the Nazi Party?

2 Read Source F. Do you think the writer was telling the truth? Was it easy for Nazis to control people's thoughts? Explain.

3 Study Source G. What did the Nazis want children to think after they had read this book? Why did the Nazis want to persuade children?

4 **Propaganda** twists the truth in order to persuade people. Are any of these three sources propaganda? Explain.

Nazi Terror

violence **Concentration Camps**

There were many Germans who did not agree with the Nazis. Hitler ordered violence and bloodshed to keep them quiet.

The Nazis had their own private army of 'storm troopers' called the S.A. Their main job was to beat up anyone the Nazis saw as a threat. They broke up rival meetings. They smashed houses and shops belonging to Jews.

Source H A S.A. poster

In 1934 even Hitler was afraid that the S.A. were getting too powerful. The S.S. were a smaller Nazi group. Some of them were trained as Hitler's personal bodyguard. On 29 June, the 'night of the long knives', Hitler gave orders to the S.S. They rounded up and killed many of the S.A. leaders, more than four hundred people. Now the S.A. would do as they were told.

In the next five years the S.A. and the S.S. were very busy. They arrested thousands of people and kept them in Concentration Camps. Some were people who had been brave enough to speak out against the Nazis. Some were criminals. Many were just unlucky. They did not fit in with Nazi ideas. Jews were arrested together with anyone else the Nazis did not like. Homosexuals, homeless people, gypsies, mentally handicapped people, there was no place for them in Hitler's 'Master Race'.

In 1939 there were 132 thousand people in Nazi Concentration Camps. Inside the camps people were often treated very cruelly and many died

WORKFILE

1 Make a list of all the different ways which the Nazis used to persuade people to follow them.

2 Suppose you work for the Nazi Party in 1938. Design a poster. Frighten your enemies so that they dare not speak out against you. Refer to the S.A. or a Concentration Camp in your poster.

WORKFILE

The sources you have studied can be used to **support** or 'back up' different views of what Nazi Germany was like. For example: Source D **supports** the view that there were less people out of work in Nazi Germany.

1 Complete the table below as follows.
  a Study Statement 1 and Source A.

Does the source support the statement? If so tick the column, if not leave a blank space. The source might even disagree with the statement. If so put a cross. Repeat for Statements 2-7.
  b Statements 8 and 9 ask you to think about where the sources came from in the first place. Write T in the table if you think the statement is true, F if you think it is false.
  c Repeat for the other sources.

Sources table

Statements	Sources							
	A	B	C	D	E	F	G	H
1. Before the Nazis Germany was in a bad way.								
2. Hitler was Germany's great hope.								
3. Nazi rule was good for Germany.								
4. Nazis used violence against their enemies.								
5. Nazis were very powerful.								
6. Nazis were racist.								
7. Nazis did not try to persuade children to follow them.								
8. This source was made under Nazi control in Germany.								
9. This source is Nazi Propaganda.								

What Were the Consequences of Nazi Rule?

We have seen that the Nazis brought many changes to Germany. Many Germans felt better off under the Nazis. For some people things seemed to get better, but not for everyone. Many Germans were arrested because the Nazis saw them as enemies. People were expected to behave the way the Nazis said. Women were expected to stay at home and raise children so there were few chances for women to do important jobs in Nazi Germany. Those who disagreed with Hitler could either keep quiet or speak out and risk arrest.

Outside Germany, Hitler decided to take the land his 'master race' wanted. In 1939 he led Germany into a war which spread to include countries from all over the world. You can learn more about the war in the next few chapters.

Six years later the war was over. Millions had died in the fighting. Germany lay in ruins. Hitler killed himself. The rule of the Nazis was over.

WORKFILE

Short-term and *Long-term* effects
Draw and complete a diagram like the one below to show the effects of Nazi rule. **Short-term effects** happen within a few years. Place them nearer the event box. **Long-term effects** happen later. Place them further away from the event box. Shade long-term and short-term effects in a different colour. Start with this list of effects. Try to add one or two of your own.

- More German people got jobs.
- Many died in Concentration Camps.
- Less work chances for women.
- 'Nazi Germans' got back their pride.
- Germany fought another major war.
- Hitler killed himself.

WHAT WERE THE EFFECTS OF NAZI RULE?

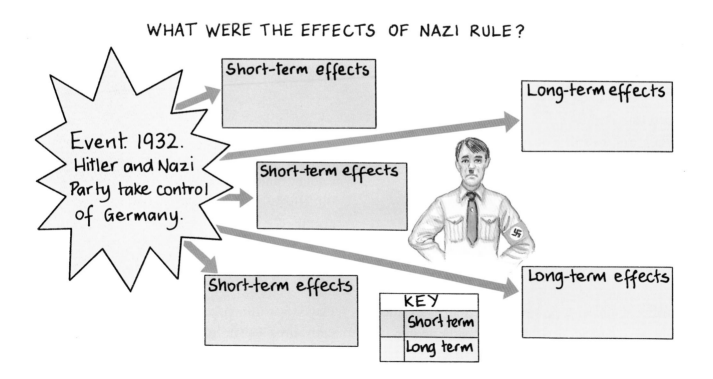

6 Why Did the Second World War Happen?

Hitler believed the Germans were a master race. They needed more land to grow stronger and richer. In the 1930s he built up the German armed forces. He used them to take control of areas of land around Europe. Some of the land had been taken from Germany by the Treaty of Versailles. Hitler reclaimed it. Some of the land belonged to other countries but German people lived there. Hitler invaded and took control.

By 1939 Germany had built up a massive and powerful war machine of tanks, planes and submarines. Too late, other countries joined forces to try to stop the Germans. The Second World War was about to begin. Play this game and learn how Hitler's power spread beyond Germany in the 1930s.

Before You Start

You will need:
- a group of three or four players
- your own token to move around the board (draw a small tank or plane.)
- your own score chart. Make a copy
- a dice or numbered papers

Aim of the Game

You should aim to 'take' all of the six areas of land on the map and at the same time build up your armed forces, measured in 'number of tanks'.

How to Play

1 Each player throws the die in turn. Use your score **either** to take land **or** to build up your number of tanks. You choose.

2 Record what happened to you on your score chart.

3 Repeat until all players have taken all six areas, then work out who has won.

Taking Land

Land areas must be taken in order, starting with number 1. To take an area you must throw that number on the die. When you have taken an area, move your token to that area. (Sometimes there may be more than one token on each area.)

Collecting Tanks

If you wish you can use your die score to collect tanks. For example, if you need area 3 but throw a 6 then add 6 tanks to your army and try for area 3 next time.

The Winner

Play stops immediately when the last player takes area 6. The player with the biggest total of tanks is the winner.

Fig 21.1. Score chart

Round	No. Thrown	Name of Land Area Taken	Tanks
A			
B			
C			
D			

WORKFILE

1 The flow chart below shows where German armies took control in the 1930s, but the events are in the wrong order. Make your own copy of the chart in the correct order and write in the dates.

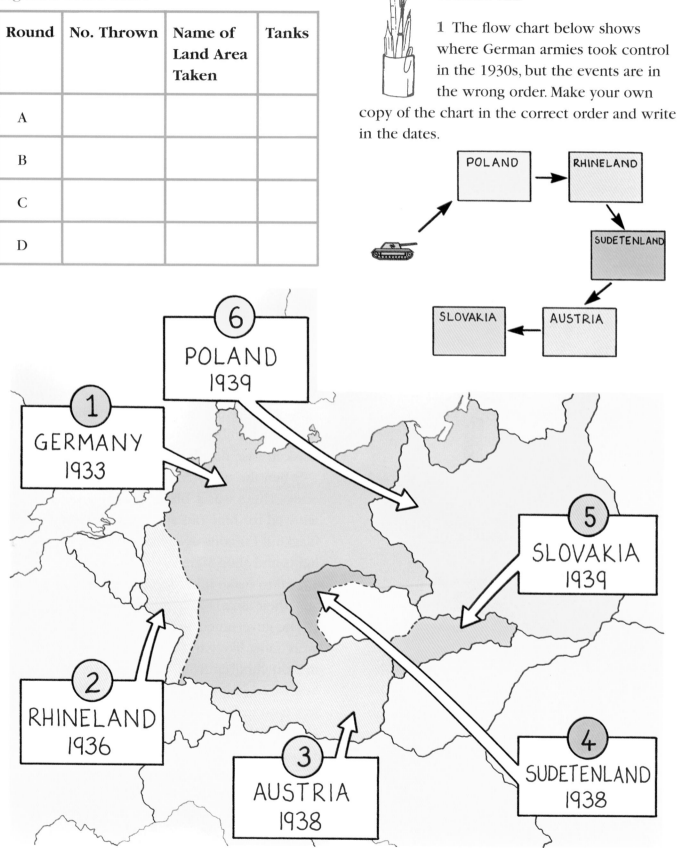

Worlds Apart: The Twentieth Century © Steve Buxton. Published by Hodder and Stoughton.

7

The Outbreak of War

conscription precautions sirens
blackout evacuated react hysterics
annihilation

The Second World War began in 1939 when Hitler's armies invaded Poland. Neville Chamberlain was British Prime Minister. On 3 September he spoke on the radio.

Source A

'... this country is at war with Germany ... We and France are going to the aid of Poland, who is bravely resisting this wicked attack on her people.'

Most people in Britain already knew war was on the way. Conscription had already started. Men aged 20 and 21 were 'called up' to join the armed forces.

Air Raids

The threat of air attacks worried many people. They expected huge air raids on British cities. Thousands of people might be killed. Several years before the war, the government planned Air Raid Precautions (A.R.P.). People volunteered to be A.R.P. wardens. They were trained to help others if there was an air raid. Warning sirens were put in place. Air raid shelters were dug where people could hide from the bombs. Everyone was given a gas mask in case the Germans dropped gas bombs.

When the war started new rules came at once. There was a 'blackout'. No lights were allowed to shine out at night. People put blackout curtains over their windows. Street lights and shop signs were switched off. They hoped to make it harder for enemy bombers to find their targets at night.

The government worked out which cities were most likely to be bombed. Nearly one million children from these cities were evacuated in just four days. They were sent to live with foster parents in country areas which were safer.

Crowds would be a problem in an air raid. How would people escape? Theatres and cinemas were closed for a while. Football games were cancelled.

The government used radio messages, leaflets, booklets and posters. They told people

Source B An artist's impression of a plane bombing Warsaw – now look at the top of the next column

This photograph shows what Warsaw actually looked like after it had been bombed

what to do and how they could help to win the war. This was a war in which everyone would take part, like it or not.

How Did People React?

How did people react to the news that Britain and Germany were at war? This person was working in a cotton factory when the news broke:

Source C

'Some believed the news, some didn't. Then one or two went out and bought a special newspaper. Then they all believed it. One weaver had hysterics. She had a son. A few were crying but on the whole they didn't bother much …'

Some German people were also worried by the idea of war. One woman living in Hamburg wrote down how she felt at the time:

Source D

'When war broke out … all those nearest to us were in despair. We were sure that total annihilation would follow right away.'

At first, the bombs did not come. For nearly a year big air raids over Britain did not happen. Cinemas opened again. Some parents ignored advice. They brought their children home, back to the cities. People forgot their gas masks.

The news from Poland though was not so good. The Germans easily beat the Polish army in just a few weeks. Then they turned their attention to France and Britain. Soon Britain had a new leader, Winston Churchill. He said, 'I have nothing to offer but blood, toil, tears and sweat.' He was Prime Minister through the rest of the war.

TALKING POINTS

1 Study Sources C and D. Why do you think people felt differently about the war? What did people expect would happen to them?

WORKFILE

1 Study the sources on the next two pages. Match the sources with the captions in the table on page 28. Write in the source letter on your copy of the table.

2 Choose two sources to study in more detail. Write a sentence or two about each one. Explain what you can learn from it.

3 Study the cartoon on page 28. What do you think these people would be thinking as they listen to the radio? Fill in the thought bubbles on your copy of the cartoon.

Source F

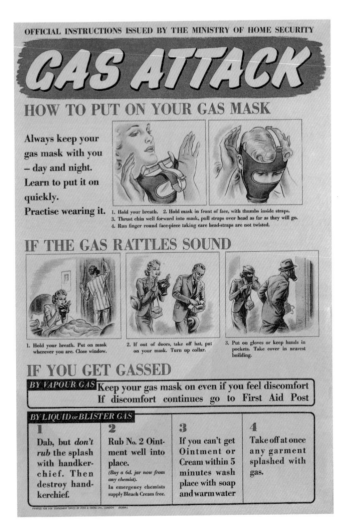

Source E

ALL SPORT BROUGHT TO A HALT

Restart When Safe for Crowds

FOR the moment all sport has been brought to a halt.

The concentration of Britain's whole effort on winning the war makes ... it unimportant.

Source G

Source H

Source J

Source I

Source K

Caption	Source
Government leaflet showing people what to do if gas bombs were dropped.	
Government poster. Asks parents to leave evacuated children in the safety of the countryside.	
Government poster. A message from new Prime Minister Winston Churchill in May 1940.	
A report from the *Daily Mail* about the ending of sports meetings. 4. 9. 1939	
Photograph of evacuated children from London arriving at their new home. They carry their gas masks in cardboard boxes.	

Worlds Apart: The Twentieth Century © Steve Buxton. Published by Hodder and Stoughton.

8 What Was it Like to Live During the War?

Living With Air Raids

> Underground sirens tension paralyse **cellar** rubble rescue

The first big bombing raid on a British city happened on 7 September 1940. The German airforce bombed London. The air raid lasted twelve hours and killed more than four hundred people. It was the start of the 'Blitz'. (See Source C.) Over the next few years the attacks went on night after night on cities all over Britain. Ordinary people were in the 'front line' of the fighting.

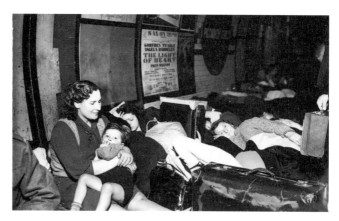

Source B These people are sleeping in a London Underground Station to escape the Blitz

Source C London during the Blitz

10 September, 1940.

Dear Jack,
The last 3 nights have been real hell! We are bombed every night. I have not had more than 2–3 hours sleep each night. I would give anything for a quiet night in the country. Everyone is tired out. They say the firemen, A.R.P. and ambulance drivers are beyond praise. The damage all along the river has been very great.
Best love, Doll.

Source D William Bush was 10 years old. He was in Liverpool when the city was bombed

'From the moment the sirens went I felt paralysed with fear, all my muscles knotting up. The relief when they started bombing. I'd scream my head off and the tension would be gone.'

Source A Bristol after the Blitz

Source E Isobel Murphy tells how she coped in an air raid shelter

'If it got really bad we started to sing as loud as we could to drown out the noise. We had the most wonderful A.R.P. warden. He stood in the doorway and said, "They won't get us down here. This cellar will keep us all safe." Then he'd start us off singing.'

Source F Bridy McHard was 11 and lived in Glasgow. The shelter she was in was hit by a bomb. Many of her family were killed but she was dug out of the rubble by a rescue team

'I came to and drifted away again. I kept shouting "Can anyone hear me?" I heard a voice saying, "We're getting to you. Don't worry." I was pulled out by the legs backwards on my face.'

Source G This woman was pulled out of the rubble alive

Many British cities suffered terrible damage. Fifty thousand people were killed. Two and a half million homes were destroyed. Many people were in despair. Their spirits sank. They lost the will to fight on. For others the bombing had the opposite effect. It made them more determined to fight on.

Later in the war the British and American airforce made big raids on German cities. (See source H below.) One German leader wrote: 'A few of us admired the British when they stuck it out in the autumn of 1940. So we have to stick it out now.'

	Bombs dropped on Britain	Bombs dropped on Germany
1940	37 K	10 K
1944	9 K	650 K
Total 1939-1945	75 K	1350 K

K = One thousand tonnes of high explosives

Source H

WORKFILE

1 How do you think you would feel in an air raid? Draw a picture of yourself in an Air Raid Shelter. Use thought bubbles to show what you would be thinking and feeling. What would you say to the others in your shelter?

2 Label the picture of an A.R.P. warden on page 31. Use these labels:
tin hat   gas mask   hand pump   rattle
whistle   torch   arm band

Write a sentence with each one. Say what you think it was used for.

3 Study Source H. Write a sentence or two to say what you can learn from the figures.

4 Complete the table on page 31. Find evidence from Sources C–E to support each statement. In the right hand column write a short quote from the evidence you have chosen.

Statement table

Statement	Source	Evidence (quote)
People escaped the bombs by going into the countryside.		
People relied on the A.R.P. for help.		
The bombs caused a lot of damage.		
Some people sheltered in cellars.		
People were tired out by the night bombing.		
People were scared by the air raid sirens.		
Some people survived a direct hit.		

Worlds Apart: The Twentieth Century © Steve Buxton. Published by Hodder and Stoughton.

imports **rations coupons Spam**
cordite routine

Rationing

Britain imports many of the things which we
need. During the war the Germans sank ships
bringing goods here. A lot of things were in
very short supply. Long queues formed outside
shops as people waited for supplies to arrive.

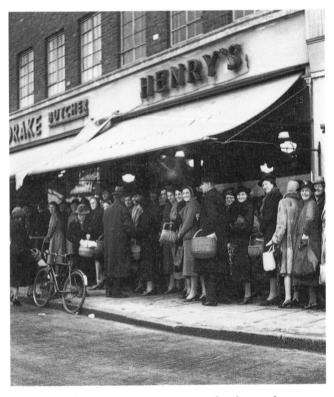

Before long the government had to take
control. They worked out what people needed
to survive. Then they issued everybody with
coupons in a 'ration book'. These said what you
were allowed to buy.

Many everyday items like food and clothing
were strictly rationed. You were only allowed to
buy small amounts. Most people accepted
rationing. At least it was fair. Even the king got
the same rations as everyone else.

People had to learn to live with much less.
Eating habits had to change. They got used to
egg powder and Spam tinned meat, dried milk
and grey bread. Broken cups and glasses were
hard to replace. Make-up and paper were hard
to find.

People looked for ways to help themselves.
The government offered advice. Posters told
people how to make the most of food. Nothing
was wasted, not even potato peelings. Many
people started to grow their own vegetables
and keep chickens. Old newspapers replaced
toilet paper. Elsie Thompson, aged 18, described
what she used for make up. Like many women,
she rubbed gravy browning on her legs to look
like stockings.

Source I

'If it rained you were in a right mess. The dogs used
to come around sniffing your legs. We put our fingers
up the chimney to get a little bit of soot to put on
our eyes and looked for long, red liquorice sweets –
that would be our lipstick.'

Working

Source J Women workers' recruitment poster 'Come into the factories'

Before the war many women worked in a shop or as a servant. Source J shows one big change which the war made to people's lives. Women were asked to do jobs which before only men had done. On factories and farms, millions of women took the place of men who were away fighting. Kitty Murphy worked in an arms factory:

Source K

'We put the caps on the bullets. You had to wear special clothing and no jewellery. The cordite used to fly about. It caused a rash in big lumps. It was very good money but you earned every penny.'

A Different Life

Was the war a good or bad time to live? Mary Bloomfield lived in Coventry. She summed up many people's feelings about the war:

Source L

'I was brave during the war. I never complained. I did what had to be done, but it was misery for 99 people out of 100. We suffered grief, but everything that happened to us we accepted. Our peaceful life was shattered. We were never the same again.'

TALKING POINTS

1 Why was Kitty Murphy's job dangerous? (Source K) Why do you think she did it?

2 How did the war change people's lives? Make a list. Which was the most important change? Why?

3 Why do you think the people in the photo who are queuing for rations look so cheerful?

WORKFILE

1 Suppose you worked for the government in 1941.
a Design a poster to tell people what their food ration is per week:
• butter – 2 ounces • cheese – 2 ounces
• eggs – 2 • milk – 1 pint • dried egg powder – 1 pkt (equal to 3 eggs) • bacon – 6 ounces
• tea – 2 ounces • sugar – 12 ounces
• sweets – 2 ounces • jam – 12 ounces
• meat worth 1 shilling (5p) • bread and vegetables, not rationed • all other food not rationed but hard to find
(1 ounce = 28 grams)

9 What Was it Like to Fight in the War?

Tanks **Blitzkrieg** fighter Jerry Panzer Sherman **bayonet grenade submarine torpedo destroyer depth charge aircraft carrier**

In 1939 the German generals made expert use of the new weapons of war. They realised that machines would be the key to winning. They made up new tactics. They attacked on the ground using large numbers of tanks backed up by planes in the sky. They called their tactics 'Blitzkrieg', lightning war. It set the pattern. In the Second World War machines were just as important as people in deciding who would win.

Control of the sky was very important. An air war often took place before any land battle. Small, fast 'fighter' aircraft tried to shoot enemy planes from the sky. Then the slower bombers could move in and attack the enemy soldiers. Source A was written by a British soldier. It describes a battle in Africa in 1942.

Source A

'The whole front leaps into life. 800 big guns fire all along the front. The whole sky is sounding with the planes going over. Our tanks show up. A number of them charge. A shooting match begins between some Jerry Panzers and British Shermans. One by one the charging Shermans are hit. Their crews leap or crawl out. Others show no signs of life. But Jerry losses are also high. Our trench is ringed by burning Panzers.'

Source B British troops move forward past a burning German tank

To capture enemy positions foot soldiers were needed. This French soldier describes fighting in Italy:

Source C

The enemy is fighting back everywhere. He is driven back with bayonets and grenades. The men are so tired they fall asleep despite the bullets. They are killed before they know it.'

Submarines played an important part in the war at sea. In the Atlantic Ocean German submarines fired torpedoes and sank many supply ships. British destroyers fought back with depth charges.

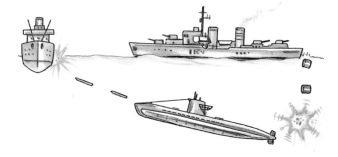

This battle went on for most of the war. A German sailor described one attack:

Source D

'Luck has been with us, a six-thousand-ton ship. We sent it to the fishes. It is so tense avoiding the destroyers and creeping up on a victim that I don't have time to think about the people on board. Just like our enemies don't feel guilty when they try to take our lives with depth charges.'

In the Pacific Ocean sea battles often involved aircraft carriers. They sent out planes to attack enemy ships.

Source E An aircraft carrier

This Japanese writer was on a carrier under attack by American planes.

Source F

'I looked up to see three enemy planes diving towards our ship. A number of black things floated slowly from their wings. Bombs! I fell to the deck. I heard the scream of the dive bombers ... a crashing explosion ... a blinding flash. The decks were bent up at all angles. Planes stood tail up in flames. Tears streamed down my cheeks.'

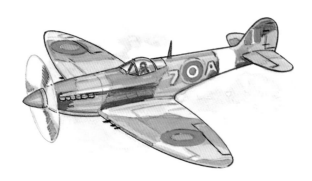

TALKING POINTS

1 How had aeroplanes changed the way war was fought?

2 Think about what you read in the last chapter. Why did the German U-Boats want to sink supply ships crossing the Atlantic Ocean?

3 If you had to fight in the war would you have been a soldier, sailor or airman. Why?

4 British women were not allowed to fight on the frontlines during the war. Why do you think this was?

5 Should both women and men be trained to fight on the frontline in the present-day armed forces?

WORKFILE

1 Draw a display of 'World War Two War Machines'. Use the pictures below to help you. Write a sentence or two with each one to say how it was used.

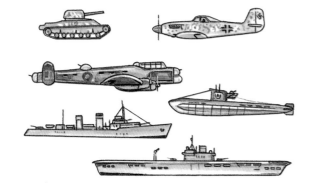

10

How Did the Allies Beat the Axis?

Allies **Axis** declared defeat Western
Eastern surrendered **advance liberated**
Marines Atomic

Find these places on your map before you start
reading: Great Britain, France, Germany, the
English Channel, Russia, Stalingrad, Pacific
Ocean, Pearl Harbor, Midway Island, Burma,
India, Japan, Imphal.

At the start of the war no one could stop the
German Blitzkrieg. The Germans took over
most of Europe very quickly. Britain was only
saved by the English Channel. Japan was just as
successful in the Far East. Japan won control of
large areas of land and millions of people. By
1941 the Axis powers, Germany, Japan and Italy
seemed hard to beat.

Then they made two mistakes. **In June 1941
Hitler's armies invaded Russia**. They wanted
to capture more land, food and oil. At first the
invasion went well. They took over vast areas
of Russia. **In December 1941 the Japanese
attacked** a U.S. navy base on an island in the
Pacific Ocean. The attack on **Pearl Harbor**
took many Americans by surprise. The
following day, **8 December 1941, the
Americans declared war on Japan**. Britain,
Russia and the United States became allies.

Now the Axis was fighting against both
Russia and America, two huge countries with
vast numbers of people who could be trained
to fight. The U.S.A. also had more factories than
anywhere else in the world. Soon they would
be turning out millions of tons of arms to defeat
the Axis.

When Were the Axis Stopped?

The Allies won several important battles to stop
the Axis advance.

**The Battle of Britain was fought between
July and September 1940**. Hitler planned to
invade Britain and started with an air attack.
The R.A.F. fought back and shot down many
German planes. Hitler had to cancel his plans.
The German advance in Western Europe had
been stopped. The small number of R.A.F. pilots
who had fought in the battle were heroes.

Stalingrad was a city in Russia. **The
Germans attacked in 1942**. It was a terrible
battle which lasted for months. Thousands of
Russian and German soldiers were killed but
the Russians would not give in. **In January
1943 the Germans surrendered**. The
German advance in Eastern Europe had been
stopped.

In **June 1942 the U.S. navy attacked the
Japanese fleet near Midway**, an island in the

Pacific. They sank four Japanese aircraft carriers with hundreds of planes on board. On land, British-led forces fought the Japanese in the jungles of Burma. **In 1944 they won a major battle at Imphal.** The Japanese advance had been stopped on land and sea.

The Defeat of the Axis

There were many bitter battles to be fought before the Allies beat the Axis. The Allied and British armies gathered in Britain. **On 6 June 1944, 'D-Day',** they crossed the Channel and landed in France. The German army tried to push them back into the sea but failed. Bit by bit the Allies liberated countries from German control. **Paris was liberated on 24 August 1944.** The Russians moved in on Germany from the East. **In May 1945 they captured Berlin.** Hitler killed himself. The war in Europe was over. Churchill declared V.E. Day (victory in Europe) on 8 May 1945.

In the Pacific the American Marines had the hard job of taking islands from the Japanese. One by one they attacked and captured many islands. The Japanese fought hard and many soldiers on both sides were killed. By 1945 the Allies had a new weapon. A bomb thousands of times more powerful than any other. Two Atomic bombs were dropped on Japanese cities. **One bomb was dropped on Hiroshima on 6 August. One bomb was dropped on Nagasaki on 9 August.** Both cities were completely destroyed. Six days later the Japanese surrendered. The Second World War ended on 2 September 1945.

WORKFILE

1 Use your copy of the world map to show how the Allies beat the Axis. Find the main events from the text. They have been written in bold type to help you. Mark as many events as you can on the map. 'D-Day' has been done for you as an example. For each one:

a Write a date to show **when** the event happened.

b Use one of the following symbols to show **what** happened.

 Battle

 Atomic Explosion

 Allies Attack

 Axis Attack

 Liberated

 Captured

 Surrendered

2 Draw a timeline to show the main events of the Second World War.

a Start with this list of events. Write down when each one happened.
Battle of Britain.   Battle of Stalingrad.
D-Day.   Atom bomb on Hiroshima.   Pearl Harbor.   End of the war.

b Then write down other important events and their dates. (Look back over the last 15 pages.)

c Sort the events into order. Design a timeline of your own. Write on the events you have collected. Use artwork to make your timeline look interesting.

3 Write a few sentences to explain why you think the Allies won the war.

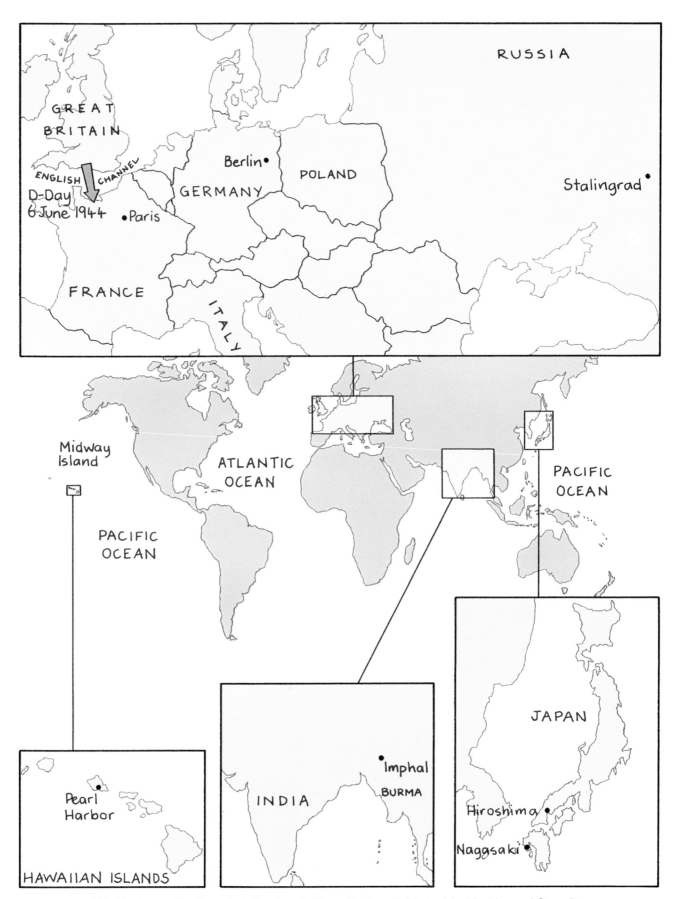

RUSSIA

GREAT
BRITAIN

ENGLISH CHANNEL

D-Day
6 June 1944

•Paris

Berlin•

GERMANY

POLAND

Stalingrad•

FRANCE

ITALY

Midway
Island

ATLANTIC
OCEAN

PACIFIC
OCEAN

PACIFIC
OCEAN

•Imphal

INDIA

BURMA

JAPAN

Pearl
Harbor

Hiroshima•

HAWAIIAN ISLANDS

Naggsaki•

Worlds Apart: The Twentieth Century © Steve Buxton. Published by Hodder and Stoughton.

What Was the Holocaust?

Concentration Camps **policy** survivors
Final Solution Holocaust deloused
memorial

Millions of people died during the Second
World War. Many were killed in the fighting but
millions more were deliberately murdered by
the Nazis. They did not fit in with how the
Nazis thought the world should be. In the
1930s the Nazis jailed thousands of Germans in
Concentration Camps. These included
handicapped people, gypsies and homosexuals.
One religious group suffered the most. They
were the Jews.

Nazis believed that some humans were less
important than others and they treated some
people as if they were hardly human at all.
When the German army marched into Russia in
1940, millions of Russian prisoners were used
as slaves. Many died because of cruel treatment.

The Final Solution

Hatred of Jews had always been a big part of
Nazi beliefs. In 1942 they began the 'Final
Solution'. They tried to arrest and kill every Jew
in Europe. Some Jews bravely tried to fight
back. Some managed to escape, often helped by
other Germans who hated the Nazis. But Nazi
soldiers still took thousands of prisoners.

They forced men and women and children
from their homes and shot them.

Source A A death squad execution

Even these methods were not quick enough
for the Nazi leaders. They decided to build
Death Camps. The one at Auschwitz could kill
two thousand people at a time. More than two
million people would die there.

Jews from all over Europe were taken there
by train. Many died on the journey. Most were
killed soon after arriving at the camp. They
were led off to showers but instead of water
they were sprayed with poison gas. The bodies
were checked for anything valuable, like gold
rings. Then they were burnt in huge ovens.

A few people managed to survive. As long as they could work they were useful to the camp guards. When they became weak, because of a lack of food, they were killed.

In 1945 Allied soldiers broke into the camps. They set free the survivors but most of them were too weak even to stand up. After the war some camp guards were put on trial. Some were hanged and some put in prison. Some escaped arrest. Some were not tracked down until the 1980s and 1990s.

What the Nazis did to the Jews and others is called 'The Holocaust'. One estimate says that around 11 million people died in the Holocaust, including six million Jews. Some of the Death Camps still stand as a reminder of one of the most tragic events in human history.

TALKING POINTS

Study and talk about this evidence about the Holocaust.

Source B The railway journey

'We lined up beside a railway cattle wagon. Once inside there is no room to sit. The door is slammed shut. A bucket is thrown in for human waste.'

Source C Jews in cattle truck

1　What can you learn from Sources B and C about the journey to the camps?

2　Why didn't the Jews refuse to go?

Source D Arriving at Auschwitz

'A S.S. officer came to meet us. He gave the order: "Men to the left, women to the right." My mother and my sister moved to the right. I walked on with my father and the other men. I was parting from my mother and sister for ever.'

3　Why do you think men and women were separated?

4　Why didn't the writer make more fuss about parting from his mother and sister?

Source E Fitness check. Drawn in secret by a prisoner

5　What do you think is happening in the picture?

6　What does the picture tell you about life in the camp?

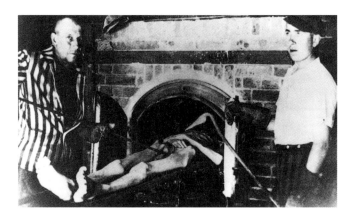

Source F The camp ovens

7 Who do you think the people loading the oven are?

8 What does the dead body tell you about life in the camp?

Source G Auschwitz

The railway carriages were unloaded. A S.S. doctor picked those fit enough to work. They were taken off to the camp.

The rest were taken to the undressing room. Men and women were separated. They were told they were to be bathed and deloused. They should leave their clothes neatly so they could find them afterwards.

Then they went into the gas chambers. These had showers and water pipes and looked like a real bath house. The door was closed and gas was let in through vents in the ceilings. Some died straight away. Others began to scream and struggle for air. In a few minutes all lay still.

Gold was taken from the teeth and hair from the women. The bodies were taken by lift up to the ovens.'

9 Why did people go willingly into the 'showers'?

WORKFILE

1 Complete the flow chart on page 42 to show what happened to prisoners at Auschwitz.

a Use these words to complete the boxes:

work   fillings   women   ovens   live   bodies   taken   weak   free   tested

b Cut and stick the boxes in the right place to complete the chart.

2 Think about the sources you have read. Complete your copy of the table opposite. Match each person in the table with the correct source.

3 Some of the Death Camps still stand as reminders of what happened. Design a memorial to display at one of the camps.

4 Write a paragraph. In your own words try to sum up what you feel about what you have read in this chapter.

TALKING POINTS

In 1948 the United Nations made a 'Declaration Of Human Rights'. The picture below shows some of its main points.

1 Why do you think they felt the need to do this at that time?

2 Which do you think is the most important Human Right? Why?

3 What 'rights' would you add to the ones below?

Children and most _____

_____ to see who could _____

stripped of clothes

_____ checked for valuables eg gold _____

Soon became _____ and ill

burnt in _____

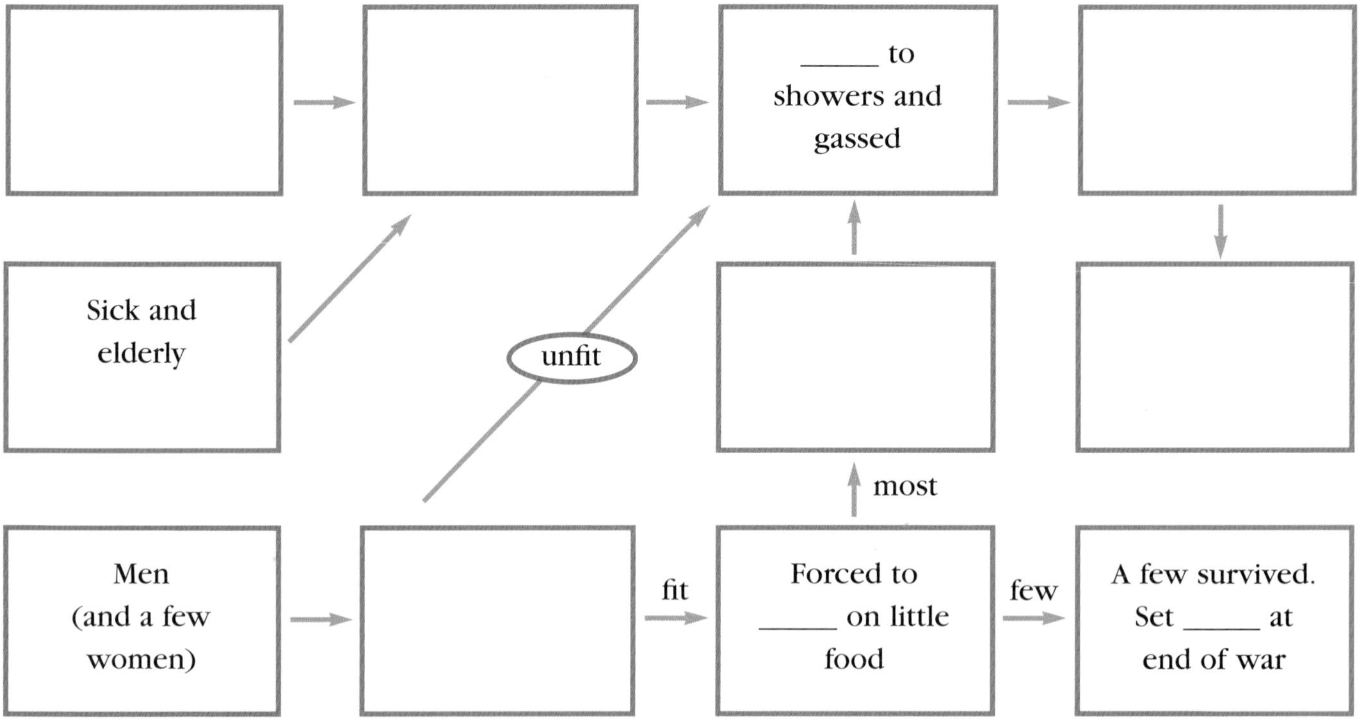

_____ to showers and gassed

Sick and elderly

unfit

Men (and a few women)

fit

Forced to _____ on little food

few

most

A few survived. Set _____ at end of war

	Source
Elie, a 15-year-old boy arriving at Auschwitz Death Camp.	
Rudolf Hoss, Commander at Auschwitz.	
David, taken by train from Poland to the Treblinka Death Camp.	

12 What Were the Effects of the Second World War?

survived **refugees welfare** debt **prefabs** N.H.S.

The Second World War was the biggest in history. Its effects were vast. More than 50 million people had been killed. At the end of the war much of Europe, Russia and Japan lay in ruins. Those who had survived now had to fight to rebuild their lives. Hard times still lay ahead.

Box No	Start	Middle	End
1	Millions of people were	buy food and weapons and owed	big problem in Europe.
2	New wartime chances gave	from the war but those in	the people and started the N.H.S.
3	American factories made money	in Britain nearly 10 years	been blown up in the fighting.
4	Britain had borrowed money to	a boost to the fight	people's way of life.
5	A new British government set	nowhere to go caused a	£6 thousand million.
6	Millions of refugees with	out to improve the welfare of	Europe were ruined or worn out.
7	Some things were still rationed	homeless because their houses had	after the war ended.
8	New wartime technology led	to big changes in	for equal rights for women.

Things were different in the U.S.A. American factories had not been bombed. Some Americans had done well out of the war. They produced and sold the food and weapons which the Allies had needed.

Study the effects chart below. It tells you about a few more effects. Some of them still affect our lives today.

WORKFILE

1 Copy the sentences from the table on page 43. First match the right start, middle and end. Use the chart below to help you. The numbers in the table tell you which box to look for in the chart.

2 Write a sentence or two in your own words. Explain which effects you think still affect our lives today.

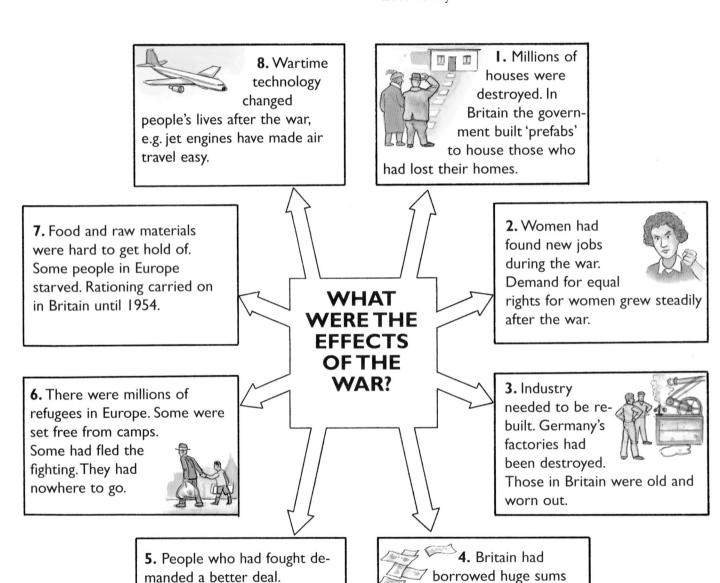

8. Wartime technology changed people's lives after the war, e.g. jet engines have made air travel easy.

1. Millions of houses were destroyed. In Britain the government built 'prefabs' to house those who had lost their homes.

7. Food and raw materials were hard to get hold of. Some people in Europe starved. Rationing carried on in Britain until 1954.

2. Women had found new jobs during the war. Demand for equal rights for women grew steadily after the war.

WHAT WERE THE EFFECTS OF THE WAR?

6. There were millions of refugees in Europe. Some were set free from camps. Some had fled the fighting. They had nowhere to go.

3. Industry needed to be re-built. Germany's factories had been destroyed. Those in Britain were old and worn out.

5. People who had fought de-manded a better deal. In Britain they voted for a new Labour government which set up the N.H.S.

4. Britain had borrowed huge sums of money to pay for the war. By 1945, Britain's debt was about £6 thousand million.

13

What Was the Cold War?

Cold War missiles

After 1945, the U.S.A. and Russia were the two most powerful countries in the world. They quickly became enemies. Both sides expected to fight each other. They said harsh words. They built up their armed forces, made more and more atom bombs and missiles. It was like a war without the fighting. A 'Cold War' which lasted until the 1990s.

Neither side dare fire the first shot. They knew it might start a Third World War which no one would survive. Both sides had enough missiles to kill everyone in the world many times over.

Source A Weapons in Russia

Europe was caught in the middle of the Cold War. Soviet soldiers were spread all over Eastern Europe after the Second World War. They stayed there for the next 45 years. Europe was split in half. Russia ruled the East. The West was friendly with the U.S.A.

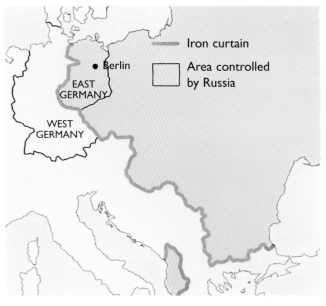

Iron curtain

Area controlled by Russia

Berlin

EAST GERMANY

WEST GERMANY

TALKING POINTS

1 On this cartoon find the Russian 'Bear' and America's 'Uncle Sam'. What are they doing? Why aren't they fighting?

2 Why is Germany looking scared?

3 When do you think the cartoon was drawn?

WORKFILE

1 Draw the cartoon. Add thought and speech bubbles for each character.

2 Write a sentence or two. Explain what the Cold War was and when it happened.

Escape From East Berlin

This game takes place in the German city of Berlin in 1961. The city is split. East Berlin is run by Russia. West Berlin is run by the U.S.A. and Britain. Many people are leaving the East side and moving to the West. Russia builds the Berlin Wall to stop people moving across.

You live in East Berlin. One family you know are desperate to escape to West Berlin. Can you help all 10 of them escape?

How to Play You will need:

- a group of three or four players
- one die per group
- your own copy of the results table

Aim

The winner is the first person to help ten people escape. You take two people on each escape attempt.

ROUND 1 Choose an escape method A, B or C. Take turns to throw the die. Use the game chart to see what happened to you. Fill in the results table.

NEXT ROUNDS Make more escape attempts. Change your method, if you wish, at the start of each round.

Results table

Round	Escape method	Die no.	How many escaped
1			
2			

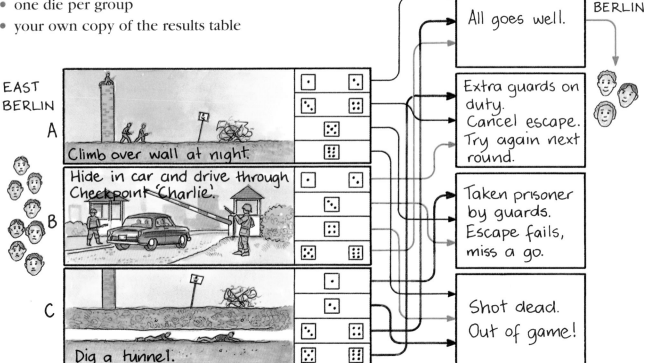

Worlds Apart: The Twentieth Century © Steve Buxton. Published by Hodder and Stoughton.

14

Did Life Improve After the War?

> rebuilding social transport engineers
> airliner **coronation** controversial
> **satellite** orbit rebellion aisles benefits

Life had been very hard for British people during the Second World War. In the next fifteen years things began to get better. There was plenty of work to do rebuilding the country so there were plenty of jobs and plenty of things to spend your wages on. More and more people could afford fashionable clothes, fridges, televisions and even cars. It was a time of great social change as people's 'way of life' began to alter.

More people could afford to run a car in the 1950s. This gave them the chance to travel more and to take holidays and day trips. The first motorway, part of the M1, was opened in 1959.

Better air transport meant some people were going even further. British engineers made the Comet, the world's first jet airliner. In 1952 the jet age arrived when the Comet went into regular service. By 1959 more than one million people a year went on cheap package holidays to 'Sunny Spain'.

In the 1930s the B.B.C. started to transmit T.V. programmes but T.V. sets were very expensive. Only the very rich could afford them. In the 1950s sets became much cheaper. The Coronation of Queen Elizabeth II was in 1953. Millions of people bought sets and tuned in to watch the black and white pictures. In the

Source A 1950s traffic jam

Source B Package holiday advert from 1950s

Source C Blackpool win the F.A. Cup in 1953

same year sport gained its first mass audience. Twelve million people saw Stanley Matthews help Blackpool win the F.A. Cup Final. When I.T.V. began in 1955 a second Channel was added. In 1962 Telstar became the first T.V. satellite. Live pictures bounced across the Atlantic Ocean from America for the first time. Television was here to stay. So was space travel. Yuri Gagarin became the first man in space on 12 April 1961. He made one orbit of the earth in his Russian spacecraft Vostok 1.

A more down-to-earth improvement in people's lives came with the National Health Service (N.H.S.) which began in July 1948. Now everyone, rich and poor, could enjoy good health care. Doctors found new cures and new drugs. One of the most controversial was the pill. This gave women more control over the number of children they had. Large families became less common.

The 1950s saw another important social change. Young adults and teenagers started to see themselves as something different. They had their own fashions and dressed differently to their parents. They had their own heroes and their own music. Rock and roll became the music of youth and rebellion. 'Rock Around The Clock' by the American group, Bill Haley and The Comets, reached No. 1 in Britain in 1955. It was featured in the movie *The Blackboard Jungle*. Some people danced in the aisles and some even tore up seats in cinemas up and down the country. In the next few years the world had its first rock superstar, Elvis Presley. Music was never the same again.

TALKING POINTS

1 Make a list of as many things you can find to show how life got better in the 1950s.

2 Some changes brought both benefits and **problems**. What do you think were the **benefits** and **problems** caused by the changes listed below?

motorways   jet aircraft   the pill   television

WORKFILE

1 Sort and copy this timetable of events. Put each event by the correct date.

Timetable of events

Year	Event
1948	I.T.V. began broadcasts
1950	Yuri Gagarin became the first man in space
1952	'Rock Around The Clock' makes No. 1
1953	National Health Service begins
1953	Coronation of Queen Elizabeth II
1955	First jet airliner service begins
1961	Britain's first motorway opens
1962	First satellite T.V. pictures sent via Telstar

2 Choose one of the events you have read about. Suppose you were a reporter at the event. Write a newspaper report. Tell your readers:
- what you have seen and heard
- how the event might change people's lives in the future